Contents

Before school

Chloe has new clothes for her first day at school.

Munch!

Crunch!

My First

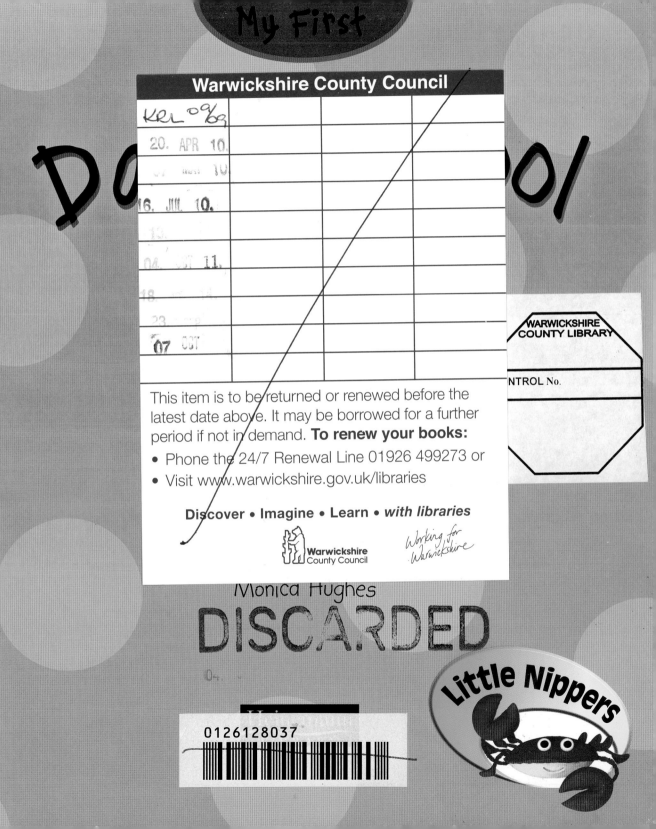

D‑‑‑‑‑‑‑‑ool

Monica Hughes

Little Nippers

www.heinemann.co.uk/library
Visit our website to find out more information about **Heinemann Library** books.

To order:
☎ Phone 44 (0) 1865 888066
🖺 Send a fax to 44 (0) 1865 314091
💻 Visit the Heinemann Bookshop at www.heinemann.co.uk/library to browse our catalogue and order online.

First published in Great Britain by Heinemann Library, Halley Court, Jordan Hill, Oxford OX2 8EJ, part of Harcourt Education.
Heinemann is a registered trademark of Harcourt Education Ltd.

Editorial: Sarah Eason and Georga Godwin
Design: Jo Hinton-Malivoire and Tokay, Bicester, UK (www.tokay.co.uk)
Picture Research: Rosie Garai and Sally Smith
Production: Séverine Ribierre and Alex Lazarus

Originated by Dot Gradations Ltd
Printed and bound in China by South China Printing Company

ISBN 0 431 18620 0 (hardback)
07 06 05 04 03
10 9 8 7 6 5 4 3 2 1

ISBN 0 431 18625 1 (paperback)
08 07 06 05 04
10 9 8 7 6 5 4 3 2 1

British Library Cataloguing in Publication Data
Hughes, Monica
Day at School – My First
372
A full catalogue record for this book is available from the British Library.

Acknowledgements
The Publishers would like to thank Gareth Boden for permission to reproduce all the photographs that appear in this book.

The cover photograph is reproduced with permission of Gareth Boden.

The Publishers would like to thank Philip Emmett for his assistance in the preparation of this book. We would also like to thank all the staff and pupils at Sheen Mount Primary School, East Sheen and Livingstone Primary School, Barnet.

Every effort has been made to contact copyright holders of any material reproduced in this book. Any omissions will be rectified in subsequent printings if notice is given to the Publishers.

Lenny is excited, but also a bit nervous.

In the cloakroom

Chloe finds out where to hang her coat.

Lenny finds his classroom.

In the classroom

Chloe can read her name on the drawer.

Lenny's teacher is called Mrs Rowe.

9

Everyone is busy

We've never seen a book that **big** before.

Lenny's class has lots of different coloured felt pens.

Playtime

Chloe's friend shows her where the toilets are.

Lenny plays outside with his friends.

Back to the classroom

Chloe is thinking hard about her numbers.

School is fun!

Lunchtime

Chloe is hungry – and ready for her lunch!

Don't the hot dinners look good?

Mmm!

Afternoon activities

See how the water swirls and splashes.

Do you like painting?

19

The day ends

Chloe is choosing a book
from the library.

Do you like singing **action** songs?

Home time

Bye-bye, I'll see you all tomorrow.

Grace   Alex

23

Index

The end

Notes for adults

This series supports the child's knowledge and understanding of their world, in particular their personal, social and emotional development. The following Early Learning Goals are relevant to the series:

- respond to significant experiences, showing a range of feelings where appropriate
- develop an awareness of their own needs, views and feelings and be sensitive to the needs and feelings of others
- develop a respect for their own cultures and beliefs and those of other people
- manage their own personal hygiene
- introduce language that enables them to talk about their experiences in greater depth and detail.

Each book explores a range of different experiences, many of which will be familiar to the child. It is important that the child has the opportunity to relate the content of the book to their own experiences. This will be helped by asking the child open-ended questions, using phrases like: How would you feel? What do you think? What would you do? Time can be made to give the child the chance to talk about their worries or anxieties related to the new experiences.

Talking about school
Starting school is a big step in a child's life and it can be made easier if the child knows their way around the building, has met other new children and knows the name of their teacher. It also helps if they are able to dress/undress independently. The child may find a full day very tiring and needs reassurance that 'home' will be there at the end of the day.

Further activities
These could include setting up a classroom for toys with the child in the role of teacher. A parent can also become a pupil. The child can help make a list of the things that need to be taken to school on different days.

Contents

Introduction

The Bible contains many wonderful stories about all sorts of people – kings, queens, soldiers, prophets and ordinary men and women. Some of these people are weak and wicked, and others are generous and strong. This book tells their stories.

The stories follow the order of the Bible – roughly the order in which the events are thought to have happened. So, if you don't know much about the Bible, read from the beginning to find out the whole story. But if you want to find out about particular people, find their names in the index on pages 62 and 63. If you come across a word you don't understand, look it up in the glossary on page 64.

Some stories in the Bible are sad. They are about illness, anger, punishment and death. Others are full of love, courage and faith. All have an important purpose, strengthening people's faith in God.

Editor: Hannah Wilson
Design: Mike Buckley and Jane Tassie
Production: Jo Blackmore
DTP Manager: Nicky Studdart
Artwork Archivists: Wendy Allison and Steve Robinson

Special thanks to our Bible Consultant, Annette Reynolds at AD Publishing Services

The publishers would like to thank the following artists for their contribution to this book:

Harry Bishop; Gino D'Achille (*Artist Partners Ltd*); Richard Garland; Rob Hefferan (*Advocate*);
John Keay; Michael Langham Rowe; Massimiliano Longo (*Milan Illustrations Agency*);
Kevin Maddison; Chris Molan; Rob Perry (*Advocate*); Francis Phillipps;
Martin Reiner; Nick Spender (*Advocate*); Roger Stewart

KINGFISHER
Kingfisher Publications Plc,
New Penderel House,
283–288 High Holborn,
London WC1V 7HZ

www.kingfisherpub.com

First published by Kingfisher Publications Plc in 2002
This paperback edition first published in 2005
2 4 6 8 10 9 7 5 3 1

1TR/0605/LFG/FR(PICA)/150MA/F

A CIP catalogue record for this book is
available from the British Library.

ISBN 10: 0 7534 1249 7
ISBN 13: 978 0 7534 1249 7

Printed in China

Places in the Bible

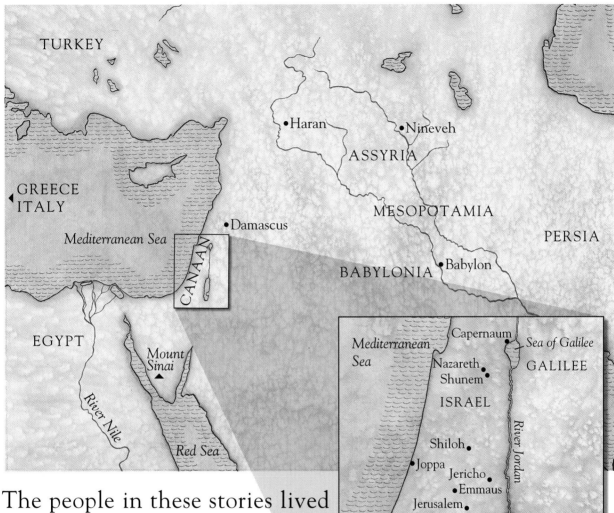

THE LAND ONCE CALLED CANAAN

The people in these stories lived in Egypt and the countries we now call Israel, Jordan, Turkey, Syria, Iraq and Iran. Of course, place names and borders change over the years, but the maps on this page provide a basic guide to the area. When you come across a place name, such as Canaan or Judea, in a particular story, look at these maps to discover where the events took place.

God

In the beginning, God created the universe. Before that, there was nothing but darkness and swirling waters.

On the first day, God made day and night. On the second, God made the sky. On the third day, God made the sea and the land, and ordered plants to grow. On the fourth day, God made the sun, moon and stars. On the fifth, God filled the seas with fish and the skies with birds. On the sixth day, God created all the animals on the land, and men and women, too. Now the creation was complete, and on the seventh day, God rested.

God was pleased with the creation, and loves and cares about Earth and all its many creatures.

From time to time, God has appeared to people – sometimes as a column of fire, or as thunder or a flash of lightning. God appeared to Moses from a burning bush. But most of all, God appeared in the person of Jesus.

God looks after the creation in three different ways – as the Father, who made human beings and loves them; as the Son, Jesus, who died to save people from their sins and then rose again; and as the Holy Spirit, who gives power to human beings, allowing them to live holy lives. In these ways, God loves and cares for every living creature.

Adam and Eve

Adam and Eve were the first people to be created by God. God put them in a beautiful garden full of wonderful fruit trees in a land called Eden.

God told Adam and Eve to care for all the living things in the Garden of Eden. God said they could eat any fruit in the garden except the fruit from the Tree of Knowledge. If they ate this, they would die.

An evil snake tempted Adam and Eve to taste the forbidden fruit, telling them that it would make them wise.

The moment Adam and Eve ate the fruit, they saw that they were naked. God soon discovered what they had done and was angry at their disobedience. God clothed them in animal skins and told them they must leave the garden. From then on, Adam and Eve had to work hard to feed themselves until the day they died.

Cain and Abel

Adam and Eve had two sons, who were named Cain and Abel. The two men were different and did different jobs. Cain liked to grow crops, but Abel preferred to keep sheep.

They were both successful in their jobs, so Cain and Abel wanted to thank God by offering a gift. Abel sacrificed his first-born lamb. Cain offered a bundle of wheat. God saw into Abel's heart and accepted his gift. God saw into Cain's heart and did not accept his gift. This made Cain so jealous and angry that he killed his brother.

When God asked Cain where Abel was, Cain pretended not to know. But God knew that he had murdered his brother, and so cursed him.

Cain could never grow crops again and had to wander the earth alone.

Noah

Noah lived at a time when people were so wicked that God decided to destroy everyone. But Noah was a good man, and God wanted to save him. God told Noah to build an ark, a huge boat, that was big enough to hold all his family and two of every kind of creature. Noah obeyed.

When everyone was on the ark, it started to rain. It rained for 40 days and 40 nights. Flood waters covered the world and every living creature drowned.

When the rain stopped, Noah sent a dove from the ark. It returned with an olive branch in its beak. Noah knew that the waters had gone down and that he could leave the ark soon. God promised that the world would never be flooded again and sent a rainbow as a sign of this promise.

Abraham

When Abraham was
an old man living
in Haran, God told him
to take his family to
the land of Canaan,
promising that he
would become the father
of a great nation. Abraham
set out on the long journey
with his wife, Sarah, and eventually
they settled in Hebron in Canaan.

In time, Sarah gave birth to a son
and named him Isaac. Many years later, God decided
to test Abraham by asking him to kill Isaac as a sacrifice.
Abraham loved Isaac, but he trusted God and wanted
to obey the order. Just as he was about to kill the boy
on a mountain-top, an angel sent by God stopped him.
Abraham sacrificed a ram instead.

God had tested Abraham's faith and knew that
it was strong. God blessed him, his son and
all his descendants – the nation of people
who later were known as the Israelites.

Lot

Lot was Abraham's nephew. He had travelled to Canaan with Abraham and Sarah, but he had settled in a place called Sodom, not far from the city of Gomorrah.

The people of Sodom and Gomorrah were very wicked, and God decided to destroy them. But first, God sent two angels to Sodom. Lot invited them into his house and the angels warned him to leave the city as it was about to be destroyed. They led Lot, his wife and their two daughters out of Sodom and ordered them not to look back.

Suddenly, balls of fire and burning stone rained down on Sodom and Gomorrah. Lot and his daughters hurried on to safety, but his wife took one last look behind her. She had disobeyed the angels and was turned into a pillar of salt.

Isaac and Rebecca

Isaac was the son of Abraham and Sarah. When Isaac was a young man, Abraham wanted to find a wife for him – someone who came from Mesopotamia, the land of his birth. So he asked a servant to travel there to find one. The servant's task was very important, but Abraham explained that God would guide him. So the servant set off for Abraham's birthplace.

When he arrived in Mesopotamia, the servant waited by a well, where young women were drawing water. One of them, a girl called Rebecca, offered him a drink of water. The servant knew that this was a sign from God and that Rebecca should be Isaac's wife.

The servant told Rebecca his story, and she agreed to return with him to Canaan. Isaac fell in love with her, and they were soon married. In time, they had twin boys – Esau and Jacob.

Jacob

Jacob was the son of Isaac and Rebecca. His twin brother, Esau, had been born first and was his father's favourite child. But Rebecca loved Jacob very much. When Isaac was an old man, Jacob and Rebecca tricked him into giving Jacob the blessing meant for the first-born. Esau was so angry about this that Jacob ran away. He travelled all day, and when the sun set, he lay down to sleep, resting his head on a stone.

That night, Jacob had a dream. He saw angels going up and down a stairway between the ground and Heaven. In the dream, God spoke to Jacob, saying, "I am the God of Abraham and Isaac. The land on which you sleep will be yours, and I will look after you wherever you go."

The next morning, Jacob poured oil over the stone that had been his pillow and dedicated the spot to God. He promised God, "If you protect me, you will be my God."

Joseph

Joseph was the son of Jacob and his wife Rachel. Jacob loved Joseph dearly and often spoilt him. This made his brothers jealous, so they sold him as a slave.

Joseph was taken to Egypt where he worked for Pharaoh. Although Joseph was honest, he ended up in prison. Here, with God's help, he interpreted the other prisoners' dreams.

One day, Pharaoh had a puzzling dream – seven fat cows were eaten by seven thin cows. Pharaoh sent for Joseph, who explained what the dream meant – there would be seven years of plenty, then seven years of famine. Pharaoh listened to Joseph and put him in charge of storing food.

Everything happened as Joseph had said. During the famine, Joseph's family came to Egypt for food. Their descendants, the Israelites, settled there for many years.

Moses

Moses was the son of an Israelite woman. Many Israelites lived in Egypt, but their lives were hard because Pharaoh used them as slaves. One day, fearing that the Israelites might rise up against him, Pharaoh ordered all Israelite baby boys to be killed. Moses' mother put him in a basket among the reeds of the River Nile. There, he was found by Pharaoh's daughter, who took him home.

Moses was brought up in Pharaoh's palace, but he always cared about the Israelites. In time, God helped him to rescue them from Egypt and lead them back to Canaan.

It was a long journey, and as they passed Mount Sinai, God called Moses to the top of the mountain. There, God gave him two tablets of stone on which the Ten Commandments were written. These were the laws that God wanted the Israelites to obey.

Joshua

Joshua was one of the Israelites who travelled out of Egypt with Moses. The journey lasted many years, and Moses grew old and frail. Before he died, God guided him to choose Joshua as the Israelites' new leader.

When the Israelites finally reached Canaan, Joshua wanted to capture the city of Jericho, but it was surrounded by strong city walls. God told Joshua what to do and he followed the instructions carefully.

On each of the following six days, Joshua marched once around the city with his army and with seven priests. The priests carried trumpets made of ram's horn.

On the seventh day, he marched his men around the city seven times. Then the priests blew on their trumpets, and the soldiers shouted loudly. Suddenly, the mighty walls of Jericho crumbled to the ground.

Deborah

Deborah was a prophet who was chosen by God to help the Israelites during a difficult time. God's people had turned away from God and their lives were very hard. They were treated cruelly by Jabin, the King of Canaan.

Deborah's task was to rescue the Israelites and help them return to God. Deborah did everything that God asked her to do. She sent for a man called Barak and asked him to gather an army of ten thousand men to fight King Jabin. Barak was willing to do this as long as Deborah agreed to help.

King Jabin's army had 900 chariots made of iron and was led by a great general called Sisera. But with God's help, Barak and Deborah got the better of him. They forced Sisera and his men onto marshy ground, where their chariots got stuck in the mud. Then they pushed his army into a narrow valley and defeated it. The Israelites were free at last.

Gideon

After many years of living in peace in Canaan, the Israelites found themselves under attack from a people called the Midianites.

God sent an angel to a man called Gideon and told him to destroy the Midianites. Gideon was only a timid farmer, but he trusted God and immediately raised a huge army. God helped Gideon to choose the best 300 men to go into battle. Under cover of night, Gideon and his men made a surprise attack. They blew trumpets made of ram's horn and waved burning torches. The Midianites panicked and began to fight among themselves. The Israelites were soon victorious, and the victory was God's.

Samson

Samson was dedicated to God from birth. He was a strong and mighty warrior. He once killed a lion with his bare hands. The Philistines, the Israelites' greatest enemy, hated him.

Samson loved Delilah, a Philistine woman. She tried to discover the secret of his strength. When he told her that it lay in his hair, Delilah betrayed him and had it cut off. The Philistines seized Samson and blinded him, and then threw him into prison.

Months later, the Philistines held a banquet. They sent for Samson to make fun of him. By this time, his hair had grown. With a prayer to God, he pushed over two stone pillars so that the roof of the hall fell in. Samson and all the Philistines were killed.

Ruth and Naomi

Ruth lived in a place called Moab. She married a young Israelite who had travelled there with his family. Sadly, he died, along with his brother and father, leaving his mother, Naomi, alone in a foreign land.

Naomi decided to return to her home town of Bethlehem. She told Ruth to go back to her own family, but Ruth loved Naomi and wanted to look after her. She told Naomi, "Wherever you go, I will go. Your people will be my people, and your God will be my God."

Back in Bethlehem, life was hard. Ruth worked in the fields, collecting grain for food. The land was owned by a kind farmer called Boaz. Ruth and Boaz married and had a son, who many years later became the grandfather of David, Israel's greatest king.

Samuel

When Samuel was born, he was the answer to the prayers of his mother, Hannah. She had begged God to give her a son and had promised to offer his life to God. So when Samuel was still only a boy, Hannah sent him to the temple at Shiloh, and he became servant to the priest, Eli.

One night, when Samuel was trying to get to sleep in the temple, he heard someone calling his name – once, twice, three times. He thought it was Eli calling, but Eli told him that the voice was God's. God told Samuel that he would become the priest at Shiloh after Eli died.

Samuel was always guided by God. He grew up to be a great priest and prophet, and everything he said turned out to be true. The Israelites trusted him so much that they asked him to choose a king for them. With God's help, Samuel chose Saul.

Saul

Saul was the first king of the Israelites. He was still only a young man when the prophet Samuel anointed him by pouring oil over his head. The ceremony was a sign that Saul had been chosen to be a future king.

At first, Saul was a good king, but then he began to ignore God's wishes. In time, God lost patience with him and told Samuel to look for a new king. Secretly, and with God's help, Samuel anointed a shepherd-boy called David. He would be the next king.

David was a wonderful harp-player, and when Saul heard him playing, he made David his personal servant. Saul loved David, but soon became jealous of him. He tried to have David killed, but he never succeeded.

Eventually, Saul died in battle, fighting the Philistines.

David

When David was a young shepherd-boy, he was handsome and very brave. He made a sling and practised firing stones so that he could defend his sheep against lions and bears.

At this time, King Saul was fighting the Philistines. One of their soldiers was Goliath, a mighty giant who carried a huge sword and a spear as thick as a tree. Goliath challenged any Israelite to fight him. David trusted God and so he volunteered.

He collected five pebbles from a stream, picked up his sling and went to face Goliath. He told the giant, "Because I have God on my side, I have the power to kill you." And with one shot from his sling, he did.

Years later, after Saul died, David became king. He captured Jerusalem and made it the capital. He became Israel's greatest ruler.

Solomon

Solomon was the son of David and Bathsheba. He became king after David's death. He ruled over Israel for 40 years. During this time, the country was at peace, and the people were happy and safe.

Early in Solomon's reign, God spoke to him in a dream and offered him a gift. Solomon asked God for wisdom so that he could rule his people well. God was pleased with this answer, so he gave Solomon not only wisdom, but riches and long life, too.

Solomon built a great temple to God. It was made of the finest stone, wood and precious metals and it stood in the centre of Jerusalem.

One day, the Queen of Sheba heard about Solomon's fame and decided to visit him. When she saw his riches and wisdom, she praised God for loving Israel and for choosing such a fine king.

Elijah

Elijah was a prophet. He lived at a time when the Israelites were ruled by a wicked king called Ahab. One day, Elijah spoke fearlessly to Ahab, telling him that God was angry and would punish him by sending a drought. Ahab was furious and did not believe a word that Elijah said.

But the prophet's words turned out to be true. There was a drought, and food became scarce. God looked after Elijah, sending him to live in the wilderness next to a stream.

Each day, God sent a flock of ravens to carry him scraps of food. In time, the stream dried up, and God sent Elijah to a nearby town to shelter at a widow's house. All she had was a cupful of flour and a few drops of olive oil. Yet, for all the time Elijah stayed with her, the food never ran out.

Elisha

Elisha was chosen by God to follow Elijah as a prophet. In his lifetime, Elisha performed many miracles, and one of these took place in the city of Shunem. There was a woman who always welcomed Elisha and gave him a room for the night. One day, he wanted to thank her for her kindness and so he told her that she would have a child. She was overjoyed when, twelve months later, she gave birth to a son.

But her joy was short-lived. When the boy was still very young, he suddenly fell ill and died. She lay his lifeless body on Elisha's bed and then set off to find the prophet. Elisha returned with her at once to Shunem. He knelt beside the child's body and prayed for him.

All at once, the boy grew warm and – atishoo! – he suddenly sneezed. Miracle of miracles – the child was alive!

Jonah

Jonah was a prophet. One day, God told him to go to the city of Nineveh, where the people were breaking God's laws. Jonah had to tell them to change their ways. But he didn't want to go, so he boarded a ship to get away.

Out at sea, there was a dreadful storm. Jonah knew that it was punishment from God for his disobedience. He told the crew to throw him overboard. The moment they did, the wind dropped, and the sea grew calm.

Jonah thought he was going to drown, but then a great fish swallowed him up. He spent three days and three nights inside the fish, and then he was spat out near the shore. Jonah thanked God he was still alive! He went straight to Nineveh. He warned the people to obey God's laws or be destroyed. The people listened to him and were sorry. They returned to God.

Isaiah

Isaiah was a great prophet, but there was a time when he thought he wasn't good enough to be one of God's messengers. "I am a sinful man," he said. Soon after, an angel visited him and told him that his sins had been forgiven.

During the time of Isaiah, the Israelites were slaves to the king of Assyria, and their lives were very hard. Many of them felt so hopeless that they turned away from God. Isaiah told them that God was angry and that the future would be even worse if they disobeyed God's laws.

Isaiah was a great speaker and, as well as blaming his people, he also tried to comfort and inspire them. He told them that Israel would be great again. He said that one day a baby would be born who would grow up to be a great leader. Isaiah called this leader the Messiah and told the people that he would bring peace to everyone on Earth. By talking about a brighter future, he gave his people hope.

Josiah

Josiah became king when he was just eight years old. His father and grandfather had been king before him, but they had disobeyed God. Under them, the people had worshipped false gods.

Josiah wanted his people to return to God. First, he got rid of the false priests and destroyed their statues and altars. Next, he began to rebuild Solomon's temple, which had fallen into disrepair. During the work, a priest discovered some ancient books. They contained the Ten Commandments – the laws that God gave to Moses.

Josiah read the laws to his people, and as he spoke, his face grew pale. He knew that his people had broken these laws and faced a fearful punishment. Josiah promised to keep God's laws all his life. For this, God did not punish the people until the king died.

Jeremiah

Jeremiah was a prophet who lived in Jerusalem when many people were wicked and selfish. They worshipped false gods and were heartless to the poor.

Jeremiah knew that God was angry and he warned the people of the danger ahead. He told them that they would be severely punished unless they changed their ways. But the people attacked and beat him, and refused to listen to what he said.

Poor Jeremiah – he trusted God and knew that his words would come true. He said that Jerusalem would be attacked and captured, and the people would become slaves. His words angered the king, who threw Jeremiah into a dark, muddy well. But some days later, he was rescued by friends, who pulled him out with ropes. Jeremiah survived to see his prophecies come true.

Shadrach

Shadrach and his two friends Meshach and Abednego worked at the royal court in the kingdom of Babylon. One day, the king, Nebuchadnezzar, built a huge golden statue and ordered everyone to bow down to it. Those who did not would be burned alive.

Shadrach, Meshach and Abednego worshipped the God of Israel so they refused to bow down to this false idol. Nebuchadnezzar ordered them to be thrown into a furnace. As the king watched, he saw that the flames didn't harm them. To his amazement, he saw a fourth figure standing next to them – it was an angel sent by God to protect the men from harm.

The king instantly freed the men and ordered everyone to respect the God of Israel.

Daniel

When Jerusalem was attacked
by the Babylonians, Daniel
was taken to Babylon to
work at the royal court.
He was a good worker
and, in time, he became
a minister to King Darius.

Some people were
jealous of Daniel's success.
Knowing that he prayed to the God of Israel,
they persuaded Darius to pass a new law. It ordered that
no one should pray to any god or man, but only to the king.
Those who disobeyed this law would be thrown into
a lions' den.

But Daniel would pray to no one but God. His enemies
caught him and took him to the king. Darius was upset
at the thought of losing Daniel, but he had to obey the law.
That evening, Daniel was thrown into the lions' den.

Next morning, to everyone's amazement,
Daniel was safe and sound. An angel had protected him
all night long. Darius was overjoyed. He rounded up
Daniel's enemies and threw them to the lions instead.

Ezekiel

Ezekiel was a priest and a prophet. Like many of the other Israelites, he had been taken to Babylon after the capture of Jerusalem. The news from their homeland was very bad – Solomon's temple had been destroyed, and Jerusalem lay in ruins. The Israelites were in despair.

Ezekiel wanted to comfort the people and give them hope, so he told them about a vision he once had. God had shown him a valley full of bones. Ezekiel told the bones that God could breathe new life into them. As he spoke, there was a great rattling sound – all the bones joined together and were covered in flesh.

Ezekiel explained to the Israelites that they could be like these bones. If they were good and obeyed God's laws, God would give them back their freedom and their land – in other words, their life.

Nehemiah and Ezra

Nehemiah and Ezra helped the Israelites after their return to Jerusalem. The people faced a difficult time, and parts of the city were still in ruins. Nehemiah wanted to help by rebuilding the city walls. One night, he visited the ruins and decided what repairs were

needed. It was a huge job, but Nehemiah inspired the Israelites and the work was finished quickly.

Nehemiah restored the Israelites' city, but it was Ezra who restored their faith. A scholar and a priest, he understood all the laws that God had given Moses. Many of the Israelites had forgotten these laws, so Ezra called everyone together and explained them from beginning to end – it took him about eight hours! The entire city felt pure and whole again, and ready to make a new start.

Esther

Esther was a beautiful Jewish woman who lived in Persia. One day, Xerxes, the king of Persia, decided to make her his queen. He thought she was Persian, but Esther was a Jew.

King Xerxes had a minister called Haman who wanted everyone to bow down to him. Esther's cousin Mordecai refused because he was also a Jew and would only bow down to God. Haman decided to punish Mordecai and every Jew in Persia. He went to Xerxes and tricked the king into agreeing to kill the Jews.

Mordecai asked Queen Esther to beg her husband for mercy. She was very frightened, but agreed to try. She invited Xerxes and Haman to a wonderful dinner, and then told the king about his wicked minister's plans. Bravely, she begged her husband to spare her life and those of her people.

Xerxes loved Esther and wanted her to be happy. He saw how Haman had tried to trick him and sent him to his death.

Job

Job was a rich farmer.
He was a good man, who
worked hard, cared for
his family and faithfully
worshipped God.
But one day, everything
changed. He lost his
animals and his
children were killed,
and boils appeared
all over his body.

Job wondered why he was being punished in this way.
His three friends tried to explain it – he must have done
something wrong. Job knew this was untrue and begged
God to tell him why he, an innocent man, should suffer.

Suddenly, out of a whirlwind, God spoke to Job,
"Who dares to challenge my wisdom and power?
Where were you when I made the world, Job?"

When Job heard these words, he understood that
God was all-powerful. He should simply have faith
in God. This pleased God so much that Job was blessed
with a new family, great wealth and a long life.

Mary

Mary lived in Nazareth in Galilee, and was engaged to a carpenter called Joseph. One day, the angel Gabriel visited her and told her that she would have a baby who would be the Son of God. Mary was amazed, but put her trust in God.

Months later, when the baby was due, an order went out telling everyone to go to their birthplace so they could register to pay taxes. So Mary and Joseph loaded a donkey and travelled to Bethlehem in Judea.

When they arrived, the town was so busy that they could find nowhere to stay. An innkeeper offered them a stable. That night, Mary gave birth to a baby boy. She called him Jesus and placed him in a manger. Later, some shepherds came to visit Jesus. An angel had told them about his birth.

Simeon and Anna

Simeon was a very old, very holy man who lived in the city of Jerusalem. He had been promised by God that, before he died, he would see the Messiah – the leader who Isaiah had prophesied would save Israel and the world.

One day, Simeon was visiting the temple, when Mary and Joseph brought in baby Jesus to be blessed. Simeon knew instantly that this was the Messiah. He took Jesus in his arms and praised and thanked God. "He will be like a light guiding the people of Israel and of every nation of the world," Simeon said.

A prophet called Anna was also in the temple. She was very old, and spent most of her time fasting and worshipping God. Anna, too, recognized Jesus as the Messiah. She was overjoyed and, after thanking God, she began to spread the news around Jerusalem.

Herod

At the time when Jesus was born, Herod was governor of Judea. He was a clever, ruthless man who enjoyed power.

One day, he was visited by wise men from the East. They told him they were following a star. It would lead them to a baby who had been born in Bethlehem and who would one day become king of the Jews. They were carrying presents for the baby – gold, frankincense and myrrh.

Herod was worried – he did not want a new king growing up in his land. He asked the wise men to come back and tell him exactly where the child could be found.

The wise men were delighted when they found Jesus, but they were warned in a dream not to return to Herod.

Herod was furious when they failed to appear and ordered all the baby boys in Bethlehem to be killed. But an angel warned Joseph about the danger, and he led Mary and Jesus to safety in Egypt.

John the Baptist

John the Baptist was the son of Elizabeth and Zechariah, who had been warned of his birth by an angel. They were told that one day their son would be a prophet.

John grew up to be a remarkable man. He wore a rough shirt made of camel hair, and ate nothing but locusts and honey. He was a powerful speaker, and huge crowds gathered to hear him. He told them that a great leader called the Messiah was coming and that they should prepare for him by being baptized. The ceremony of baptism could 'wash away' their sins with water, as long as these sins were truly confessed first.

One day, Jesus came to be baptized in the River Jordan. He asked John to baptize him, and John did as he asked. When Jesus rose out of the water, a dove flew down, and the voice of God was heard, saying, "This is my beloved son, in whom I am well pleased."

Jairus

Jairus was an important man
in the synagogue of Capernaum.
One day, he went to Jesus, begging
him to heal his young daughter,
who was dangerously ill. Jesus agreed.

As the two men went on their way, a sick woman
struggled through the crowd that had gathered to see Jesus.
She managed to touch Jesus' cloak and, instantly, she felt
well again. Jesus turned to face her. "It is your faith in God
that has made you well," he said.

Then Jesus and Jairus hurried on. Soon they heard news
that the girl had died, but Jesus told Jairus, "Only believe
and your daughter will be well."

When they arrived at
Jairus' house, Jesus took
the dead girl's hands
and commanded her to
get up. Immediately,
she opened her eyes.
Jairus' daughter
was healed.

Lazarus

Lazarus and his two sisters, Martha and Mary, lived near Jerusalem in a town called Bethany. They were all good friends of Jesus.

One day, Jesus heard that Lazarus was very ill. He travelled to Bethany, but by the time he arrived, Lazarus had been dead for four days. Martha and Mary were weeping for their brother. "If only you had been here sooner," they said to Jesus, "Lazarus would not have died." Jesus tried to comfort them. He said that Lazarus would live again and told them to have faith in God.

Jesus made his way to the tomb where Lazarus had been laid. He ordered the stone at the entrance of the tomb to be rolled away. Then he called to Lazarus, commanding him to come outside. Moments later, Lazarus appeared, alive and well, wearing his burial clothes. This was one of the most amazing miracles that Jesus ever performed.

Jesus

Jesus is the Son of God. He came to Earth as the Messiah to bring about God's kingdom. He was helped in his work by twelve trusted friends, the disciples.

Jesus was a wonderful teacher and told simple stories called parables. He urged people to love their enemies, and he reached out to taxmen, lepers and criminals, who were unpopular at that time.

Jesus performed many miracles. Once, after many hours preaching to a crowd of people, he realized that everyone was hungry. The only person with any food was a young boy, who had five small loaves and two fish. Jesus took the food and prayed to God. Then he gave it to his disciples to hand round. There was enough to feed more than 5,000 people.

That same evening, there was another miracle. The disciples were rowing across the Lake of Galilee when a storm blew up. They were afraid their boat would sink. They suddenly saw a figure coming towards them, walking on the water. It was Jesus. As soon as the disciple Peter recognized his master, he jumped out of

the boat and began to walk towards him. Moments later, he lost his nerve, and started sinking. Jesus reached out and pulled him up, telling him to have more faith.

Not everybody trusted Jesus. Some of the things he said and did shocked and offended people – especially priests, Jewish elders and Roman rulers. They thought he was a troublemaker, and they had him arrested and crucified.

Three days after his crucifixion, Jesus rose from the dead. Several weeks later, he ascended into Heaven and returned to God, his Father. His work on Earth was done.

Bartimaeus

Bartimaeus was a blind beggar. Every day, he sat by the side of the road that led out of Jericho and begged from the passers-by.

One day, Jesus was leaving the city. As usual, he was surrounded by a crowd, eager to speak to him and hear what he said. When Bartimaeus heard that Jesus was nearby, he started to call out his name. This annoyed many of the people in the crowd and they tried to keep him quiet. But he ignored them and went on shouting, "Jesus, have mercy on me."

Jesus heard him, and asked the people to bring Bartimaeus over. When they were face to face, Jesus asked Bartimaeus what it was he wanted. Bartimaeus replied, "I want to see." Jesus saw that his faith was very strong and instantly healed his sight. Bartimaeus was delighted. He praised Jesus and joined the crowd who were following him.

Zacchaeus

Zacchaeus was a rich tax collector. Nobody liked him because he was a crook and cheated people out of their money.

One day, Zacchaeus heard that Jesus was passing by. There was a big crowd lining the road, and Zacchaeus, who was very short, climbed a nearby fig tree to get a better view.

Soon Jesus came along. As he passed beneath the tree, he looked up at Zacchaeus and said, "Hurry down. I want to rest at your house for a while." At this, the crowd began to grumble – it was wrong for Jesus to visit the house of such a sinful man. But Zacchaeus spoke up, saying he was sorry for his sins. He promised to return four times the money he had stolen and give half his riches to the poor.

Jesus was pleased. He explained to the crowd that it was people like Zacchaeus that he had come to save.

The Twelve Disciples

Jesus had many followers. He chose twelve of them to be his trusted friends and to help him with his work. They were James and his brother John, Peter, Andrew, Matthew, Philip, Simon, Bartholomew, Thomas, James, Thaddeus and Judas Iscariot.

The twelve disciples came from different walks of life. Four of them – James, John, Peter and Andrew – were fishermen, and Matthew was a tax collector. They all left their jobs to follow Jesus because they were inspired by his words and deeds.

The more the disciples learned about Jesus, the more their faith in him grew. They believed he was the Messiah and they saw him perform many miracles.

One night, Peter, James and John saw Jesus shining brightly in the presence of the great prophets Moses and Elijah. Then they heard God call him "my Son".

During the last week of Jesus' life, there was a special Jewish festival called Passover. Jesus celebrated it by eating with his disciples in Jerusalem. It was to be their last supper together. Jesus told them that one of them would betray him to his enemies. He said, "The one I give this bread to will be the traitor." He handed the bread to Judas.

The next day, Judas led Roman soldiers to a garden where Jesus was praying and identified him with a kiss. The soldiers led Jesus away.

The disciples were greatly saddened by Jesus' death, but they continued to preach and tell people about his life.

Pontius Pilate

Pontius Pilate was the Roman governor of Judea. After Jesus was arrested in Jerusalem, he was sent to Pilate for trial. Jesus' enemies wanted him put to death. They said he was guilty of breaking Jewish law and of claiming to be king. Pilate questioned Jesus, but decided he was harmless. He suggested that Jesus should be released, but the crowd disagreed. They wanted a murderer called Barabbas to be freed instead. So, with a heavy heart, Pilate handed Jesus over to be crucified.

Jesus was stripped, and a crown of thorns was put upon his head. He had to carry a heavy wooden cross through the streets and be jeered and mocked by the crowd. At the place of crucifixion, he was nailed to the cross.
At midday, the sky overhead grew dark.
Three hours later, Jesus died.

Joseph of Arimathea

Joseph, who came from Arimathea, a town not far from Jerusalem, was an important and wealthy man. He was a member of the Jewish high court, but he was also a follower of Jesus. He kept this a secret from other Jews because the Jewish high court hated Jesus and all his followers.

After Jesus had died, Joseph went to see Pontius Pilate and asked for Jesus' body. Pilate agreed. Then, Joseph and his friend Nicodemus, who was another follower of Jesus, took down the body from the wooden cross. They rubbed it with oils and wrapped it in a linen sheet. Then they laid the body in Joseph's own family tomb – an empty cave recently dug out of the solid rock. Before they walked away, they rolled a huge, heavy stone across the entrance of the tomb.

Mary Magdalene

Mary Magdalene was a friend and follower of Jesus. She hadn't always lived a good life, but with Jesus' help, she had made a fresh start. She followed Jesus devotedly, and was near him when he died on the cross.

Two days after Jesus' crucifixion, Mary visited his tomb. But when she got there, she discovered that the tomb was empty and the stone had been rolled away.

Mary ran to fetch the disciples Peter and John, who came to see the tomb for themselves. They ran off, talking excitedly, and left Mary weeping by the tomb.

Soon, a man came up to comfort her. She thought he was just the gardener, but when he spoke her name, she realized it was Jesus! Jesus told Mary he had risen from the dead and would soon return to God in Heaven.

Cleopas

Cleopas was a follower of Jesus. A few days after Jesus' death, Cleopas and a friend were walking to a village called Emmaus, talking about Jesus' arrest and crucifixion. On the road, they were joined by Jesus, but as strange as it sounds, neither man recognized him. They all walked along together. Jesus asked why the men looked so sad. They told him all about Jesus and the heartbreaking news of his death. Jesus tried to comfort them, saying that the Messiah had to die, just as the prophets had foretold.

When the three men reached Emmaus, they decided to eat together. Jesus picked up some bread, broke it and blessed it – and suddenly, his companions knew who he was! At that very moment, Jesus disappeared. The two men were astounded, but overjoyed. They rushed back to Jerusalem to find the disciples and tell them what they had seen.

The Holy Spirit

After Jesus had ascended into Heaven
to return to God, his Father,
the disciples went to Jerusalem.
Jesus had told them to go to the city
and wait to be baptized – not with
water but with the Holy Spirit.

The Holy Spirit was God's
special gift. The Spirit would fill
them with power, allowing them to
take God's message to everyone –
whoever or wherever they might be.

At this time of year, there
was a special Jewish festival,
known as the Feast of Pentecost.
The disciples gathered together,
praying and waiting. Suddenly,
they felt a strong wind blowing
and it filled the entire room.
Then tongues of flame came down
and touched each and every one of them.
For the disciples, it was an amazing feeling
– the breath of God, the coming of the Spirit.

When it was over, they found that
they could speak many other languages.
Now they could travel and tell people
the good news that God loved them
and would forgive their sins.
Filled with this new power,
they went out into the city and
spoke to great crowds of people.
In time, they found they had
the power to heal just as
Jesus had done.
This power came
from the Holy Spirit.
The disciples could now
go out and do whatever
God wanted them to do.
It was as if Jesus was there
in person again. But now
his power was shared among
them all, allowing others
to learn and be helped by God.
With the power of the Holy Spirit,
every believer could know God
and live life according to God's way.

Stephen

Stephen was chosen by the disciples to help them spread the message of Jesus. Some Jewish people, after listening to the disciples, believed that Jesus Christ was the Messiah. These people became known as Christians. But many Jewish people did not believe this and became angry with the Christians.

Stephen was a great speaker and encouraged many people to become Christians. He explained the meaning of Jesus' death and resurrection. He said that Jesus died to save people from their sins, and rose again to show his power over death. People who believed in him would have eternal life. This shocked the Jewish leaders, who took Stephen to the Jewish high court. There, he had a vision of God and Jesus. This so angered the court that they ordered him to be stoned to death. In this way, Stephen became the first Christian martyr.

Dorcas

Dorcas was a Christian woman who lived in the town of Joppa. She was kind and helpful to the poor. One day, she fell gravely ill and died soon afterwards. Her friends were shocked and heartbroken. When they heard that Peter, the disciple of Jesus, was visiting a nearby town, they decided to send for him.

Peter came to Dorcas' house and knelt beside her bed. He prayed for a moment and then, raising his head, told her to get up. Amazingly, she opened her eyes, and sat up and looked around. She was alive! Her friends were amazed and overjoyed. They spread news of the miracle throughout the town. Many people who heard Dorcas' story became believers, and asked to be baptized.

Paul

Paul, who was first called Saul, was a Jew who followed his religion very strictly. He did not believe that Jesus was the Messiah and he hated the Christians. He wanted to stamp out their new religion and he had many of them arrested.

One day, he was travelling to the city of Damascus, when he was blinded by a bright light. He heard the voice of Jesus ask, "Saul, why are you persecuting me?"

From that moment Saul was blind. He was led into Damascus and he waited there for three days. Then Jesus sent one of his followers to restore his sight. Saul realized that Jesus was truly the Messiah, and he was immediately baptized. From that day onwards, he was known as Paul.

People were amazed at Paul's change of heart. He became the most important missionary of the new Christian church. He travelled tirelessly, spreading the word of Jesus far and wide to places such as Italy, Turkey and Greece.

Silas

Silas was a Christian and a friend of Paul, and travelled with him on many journeys. It was dangerous work being a Christian missionary, because sometimes they were seen as troublemakers.

One day, when they were in Philippi, a city in Greece, Silas and Paul were beaten and thrown into prison. In spite of this, the two men were strong and calm, and they prayed and sang to God.

That night, there was an earthquake in the city. The prison doors burst open and the prisoners' chains fell from the walls. The jailer was terrified that his prisoners had escaped and that he would be blamed. But Paul called out that they were both still there and that they would not try to escape. This greatly relieved the jailer. He could feel some power in Paul and Silas and asked to be baptized. The following day, an order arrived and the two missionaries were set free.

Timothy

Timothy was a close friend of Paul. He had a Greek father and a Jewish mother but, after listening to Paul, he decided to become a Christian. After that, he travelled widely with Paul and helped him with his missionary work.

One day, while they were on their travels, Paul preached to a roomful of people. He spoke for a very long time, continuing into the night. A young man called Eutychus, who had been trying to keep awake, fell asleep by an open window and toppled out to his death. Timothy watched as Paul rushed downstairs and cradled Eutychus in his arms. Instantly, the young man came back to life.

Timothy also went on journeys of his own, spreading the word of Jesus. He was timid at first, but Paul wrote to him often, encouraging him and praising his faith. To Paul, he was like a son – someone who would carry on his work.

Luke

Luke was a doctor, and a good friend of Paul, and helped him when he was in trouble. Paul was often accused by Jewish elders of preaching against their law. Time after time, they had him arrested. At last, he was sent to Rome to be judged by the emperor himself. Luke decided to travel with him.

During the voyage, their ship met a terrible storm and the crew feared for their lives. Paul comforted them, saying that an angel had told him that everyone would be safe.

Soon, the ship hit a sandbank and began to break up in the storm. Although they were still a long way from land, Luke, Paul and every crew member had to leap into the towering waves. Some clung to wooden planks, and others swam for the shore. But everyone escaped with his life – not a single person drowned.

Index

Main entries are in **bold type**.

Glossary

anoint	to make something or someone holy by pouring oil over it
ascension	Jesus' return from Earth to his Father in Heaven
baptize	to plunge someone in water as a sign of sin washed away
bless	to ask for God's help and protection for someone
Christians	people who believe that Jesus Christ is the Messiah, the person chosen by God, and who try to follow his teachings
crucify	to kill someone by nailing them to a wooden cross
disciple	one of twelve close followers of Jesus; sometimes called an apostle
fast	to go without food
Pentecost	a Jewish festival that celebrates the harvest and the giving of the Ten Commandments
Israelites	people who lived in Israel and who were descended from Abraham, Isaac and Jacob
Jews	the Israelites who followed God's commandments, but did not think that Jesus was the Messiah
martyr	someone who is killed because of their Christian beliefs
missionary	a person who teaches others about his or her religion
persecute	to treat someone cruelly and unfairly
Pharaoh	the ruler, or king, of Egypt
Philistines	a strong, warlike people who attacked and fought the Israelites
preach	to talk to people in order to give them religious advice
priest	a person specially chosen and trained to lead religious services
prophesy	to say what will happen in the future
prophet	someone who receives messages from God and tells other people about them
resurrection	Jesus' return from death to a new life that would last forever
sacrifice	an offering made to God
synagogue	a Jewish place of worship, study and meeting